50 BBQ Side Recipes for Home

By: Kelly Johnson

Table of Contents

- Classic Coleslaw
- Potato Salad
- Baked Beans
- Grilled Corn on the Cob
- Macaroni Salad
- Pasta Salad
- Cornbread
- Grilled Vegetables
- Watermelon Salad
- Caprese Salad Skewers
- Fruit Salad
- Deviled Eggs
- BBQ Baked Potatoes
- Garlic Bread
- Grilled Asparagus
- Stuffed Jalapeños
- Spinach and Artichoke Dip
- BBQ Tofu Skewers
- Cucumber Salad
- Grilled Pineapple
- Roasted Sweet Potatoes
- BBQ Brussels Sprouts
- Vegan Coleslaw
- Grilled Peaches with Balsamic Glaze
- Antipasto Platter
- Hawaiian Macaroni Salad
- Grilled Zucchini
- Southern Hush Puppies
- BBQ Cauliflower Wings
- Tomato and Mozzarella Salad
- Grilled Eggplant
- Cowboy Caviar (Black Bean Salad)
- Grilled Portobello Mushrooms
- BBQ Cornbread Muffins
- Broccoli Salad

- Grilled Romaine Lettuce
- Mediterranean Orzo Salad
- BBQ Potato Wedges
- Stuffed Mushrooms
- Three Bean Salad
- Grilled Bell Pepper Salad
- Corn and Avocado Salad
- BBQ Green Beans
- Grilled Okra
- Caprese Pasta Salad
- BBQ Bruschetta
- Asian Slaw
- Grilled Fennel
- Greek Salad Skewers
- BBQ Rice Pilaf

Classic Coleslaw

Ingredients:

- 1 small head of green cabbage, thinly sliced
- 2 medium carrots, grated
- 1/2 cup mayonnaise (vegan mayonnaise for vegan option)
- 2 tablespoons apple cider vinegar
- 1 tablespoon dijon mustard
- 1 tablespoon maple syrup or sugar
- Salt and pepper to taste

Instructions:

1. In a large mixing bowl, combine the thinly sliced cabbage and grated carrots.
2. In a separate small bowl, whisk together the mayonnaise, apple cider vinegar, dijon mustard, maple syrup or sugar, salt, and pepper until well combined.
3. Pour the dressing over the cabbage and carrots in the large mixing bowl.
4. Toss the coleslaw until the vegetables are evenly coated with the dressing.
5. Taste and adjust the seasoning, adding more salt and pepper if needed.
6. Cover the bowl and refrigerate the coleslaw for at least 30 minutes to allow the flavors to meld together and for the cabbage to soften slightly.
7. Give the coleslaw a final toss before serving.
8. Serve the classic coleslaw chilled as a side dish alongside your favorite BBQ meats.

Enjoy the refreshing crunch and tangy flavor of this classic coleslaw with your BBQ feast!

Potato Salad

Ingredients:

- 2 pounds (about 1 kg) potatoes (Yukon Gold or red potatoes work well), peeled and cut into bite-sized pieces
- 1/2 cup vegan mayonnaise
- 2 tablespoons Dijon mustard
- 1 tablespoon apple cider vinegar
- 1/2 cup diced celery
- 1/4 cup diced red onion
- 1/4 cup chopped fresh parsley
- Salt and pepper to taste
- Optional: chopped green onions for garnish, paprika for sprinkling

Instructions:

1. Place the peeled and chopped potatoes in a large pot and cover with cold water. Add a pinch of salt to the water.
2. Bring the water to a boil over medium-high heat. Reduce the heat to medium-low and let the potatoes simmer until they are fork-tender, about 10-15 minutes.
3. While the potatoes are cooking, in a large mixing bowl, whisk together the vegan mayonnaise, Dijon mustard, and apple cider vinegar until well combined.
4. Once the potatoes are cooked, drain them in a colander and let them cool for a few minutes.
5. Add the diced celery, diced red onion, and chopped fresh parsley to the mixing bowl with the mayonnaise mixture.
6. Once the potatoes have cooled slightly, add them to the mixing bowl with the other ingredients.
7. Gently toss the potato salad until everything is evenly coated with the dressing.
8. Taste the potato salad and adjust the seasoning, adding more salt and pepper if needed.
9. Cover the bowl and refrigerate the potato salad for at least 1 hour to chill and allow the flavors to meld together.
10. Before serving, give the potato salad a final toss and sprinkle with chopped green onions and paprika for garnish if desired.
11. Serve the potato salad cold as a delicious side dish at your BBQ.

Enjoy the creamy and flavorful goodness of this classic potato salad alongside your favorite grilled meats and veggies!

Baked Beans

Ingredients:

- 2 cans (15 oz each) of cooked beans (such as navy beans, pinto beans, or kidney beans), drained and rinsed
- 1/2 cup tomato sauce
- 1/4 cup maple syrup or molasses
- 2 tablespoons brown sugar
- 2 tablespoons apple cider vinegar
- 1 tablespoon Dijon mustard
- 1 small onion, finely diced
- 2 cloves garlic, minced
- 1/4 teaspoon smoked paprika
- Salt and pepper to taste
- Optional: vegan bacon bits or diced smoked tofu for extra flavor

Instructions:

1. Preheat your oven to 350°F (175°C).
2. In a large mixing bowl, combine the drained and rinsed beans with the tomato sauce, maple syrup or molasses, brown sugar, apple cider vinegar, Dijon mustard, diced onion, minced garlic, smoked paprika, salt, and pepper. Stir until everything is well combined.
3. Transfer the bean mixture to a baking dish or casserole dish.
4. If desired, sprinkle vegan bacon bits or diced smoked tofu over the top of the beans for extra flavor.
5. Cover the baking dish with aluminum foil and bake in the preheated oven for 45-60 minutes, or until the beans are bubbling and the sauce has thickened.
6. Remove the foil and bake for an additional 10-15 minutes, or until the top is golden brown and caramelized.
7. Once baked, remove the beans from the oven and let them cool for a few minutes before serving.
8. Serve the baked beans hot as a delicious side dish at your BBQ.

Enjoy the sweet and savory goodness of homemade baked beans alongside your favorite grilled meats and veggies!

Grilled Corn on the Cob

Ingredients:

- Fresh corn on the cob, husks removed
- Olive oil or melted vegan butter
- Salt and pepper to taste
- Optional toppings: chopped fresh herbs (such as parsley, cilantro, or chives), vegan Parmesan cheese, lime wedges

Instructions:

1. Preheat your grill to medium-high heat.
2. Brush each ear of corn with olive oil or melted vegan butter, ensuring they are well coated.
3. Season the corn with salt and pepper to taste.
4. Place the corn directly on the grill grates.
5. Grill the corn for 10-15 minutes, turning occasionally, until the kernels are tender and lightly charred in spots. Be careful not to let them burn.
6. Once the corn is cooked, remove it from the grill and transfer it to a serving platter.
7. If desired, sprinkle the grilled corn with chopped fresh herbs, vegan Parmesan cheese, or a squeeze of lime juice.
8. Serve the grilled corn on the cob hot as a delicious side dish at your BBQ.

Enjoy the smoky and sweet flavor of grilled corn on the cob alongside your favorite BBQ meats and other sides!

Macaroni Salad

Ingredients:

- 8 oz (about 2 cups) elbow macaroni
- 1/2 cup vegan mayonnaise
- 2 tablespoons apple cider vinegar
- 1 tablespoon Dijon mustard
- 1 tablespoon maple syrup or sugar
- 1/2 teaspoon garlic powder
- 1/2 teaspoon onion powder
- Salt and pepper to taste
- 1/2 cup diced celery
- 1/2 cup diced red bell pepper
- 1/4 cup diced red onion
- 1/4 cup chopped fresh parsley
- Optional: diced pickles, sliced black olives, chopped green onions

Instructions:

1. Cook the elbow macaroni according to the package instructions until al dente. Drain the cooked macaroni and rinse it under cold water to cool it down.
2. In a large mixing bowl, whisk together the vegan mayonnaise, apple cider vinegar, Dijon mustard, maple syrup or sugar, garlic powder, onion powder, salt, and pepper until well combined.
3. Add the cooked and cooled macaroni to the mixing bowl with the dressing.
4. Add the diced celery, diced red bell pepper, diced red onion, and chopped fresh parsley to the bowl.
5. Gently toss all of the ingredients together until everything is evenly coated with the dressing.
6. Taste the macaroni salad and adjust the seasoning, adding more salt and pepper if needed.
7. If desired, add diced pickles, sliced black olives, or chopped green onions for extra flavor and texture.
8. Cover the bowl and refrigerate the macaroni salad for at least 1 hour to chill and allow the flavors to meld together.
9. Before serving, give the macaroni salad a final toss to redistribute the dressing.

10. Serve the macaroni salad cold as a delicious side dish at your BBQ.

Enjoy the creamy and tangy goodness of this classic macaroni salad alongside your favorite grilled meats and veggies!

Pasta Salad

Ingredients:

- 8 oz (about 2 cups) pasta of your choice (such as rotini, penne, or fusilli)
- 1/2 cup diced red bell pepper
- 1/2 cup diced green bell pepper
- 1/2 cup diced cucumber
- 1/2 cup halved cherry tomatoes
- 1/4 cup sliced black olives
- 1/4 cup chopped red onion
- 1/4 cup chopped fresh parsley
- 1/4 cup chopped fresh basil
- 1/2 cup vegan Italian dressing (store-bought or homemade)
- Salt and pepper to taste
- Optional toppings: vegan Parmesan cheese, pine nuts, chopped green onions

Instructions:

1. Cook the pasta according to the package instructions until al dente. Drain the cooked pasta and rinse it under cold water to cool it down.
2. In a large mixing bowl, combine the cooked and cooled pasta with the diced red bell pepper, diced green bell pepper, diced cucumber, halved cherry tomatoes, sliced black olives, chopped red onion, chopped fresh parsley, and chopped fresh basil.
3. Pour the vegan Italian dressing over the pasta salad and toss everything together until well combined and evenly coated with the dressing.
4. Taste the pasta salad and season with salt and pepper to taste.
5. If desired, sprinkle vegan Parmesan cheese, pine nuts, or chopped green onions over the top of the pasta salad for extra flavor and texture.
6. Cover the bowl and refrigerate the pasta salad for at least 1 hour to chill and allow the flavors to meld together.
7. Before serving, give the pasta salad a final toss to redistribute the dressing.
8. Serve the pasta salad cold as a delicious side dish at your BBQ.

Enjoy the fresh and vibrant flavors of this classic pasta salad alongside your favorite grilled meats and veggies!

Cornbread

Ingredients:

- 1 cup cornmeal
- 1 cup all-purpose flour
- 1/4 cup granulated sugar (optional, adjust to taste)
- 1 tablespoon baking powder
- 1/2 teaspoon baking soda
- 1/2 teaspoon salt
- 1 cup non-dairy milk (such as almond milk or soy milk)
- 1/4 cup melted vegan butter or vegetable oil
- 2 tablespoons maple syrup or agave syrup (optional, for added sweetness)
- 1 tablespoon apple cider vinegar

Instructions:

1. Preheat your oven to 400°F (200°C). Grease an 8x8 inch baking dish or line it with parchment paper.
2. In a large mixing bowl, whisk together the cornmeal, all-purpose flour, sugar (if using), baking powder, baking soda, and salt until well combined.
3. In a separate bowl, mix together the non-dairy milk, melted vegan butter or vegetable oil, maple syrup or agave syrup (if using), and apple cider vinegar.
4. Pour the wet ingredients into the dry ingredients and stir until just combined. Be careful not to overmix.
5. Pour the batter into the prepared baking dish and smooth the top with a spatula.
6. Bake in the preheated oven for 20-25 minutes, or until the top is golden brown and a toothpick inserted into the center comes out clean.
7. Remove the cornbread from the oven and let it cool in the baking dish for a few minutes before slicing and serving.
8. Serve the cornbread warm as a delicious side dish at your BBQ.

Enjoy the fluffy texture and slightly sweet flavor of this classic cornbread alongside your favorite BBQ meats and sides!

Grilled Vegetables

Ingredients:

- Assorted vegetables of your choice (such as bell peppers, zucchini, eggplant, mushrooms, onions, cherry tomatoes, asparagus, etc.)
- Olive oil
- Salt and pepper to taste
- Optional seasonings: garlic powder, onion powder, dried herbs (such as thyme, oregano, or rosemary), balsamic vinegar

Instructions:

1. Preheat your grill to medium-high heat.
2. Wash and prepare the vegetables by slicing them into uniform pieces. Larger vegetables like bell peppers and eggplant can be sliced into rings or wedges, while smaller vegetables like cherry tomatoes and mushrooms can be left whole or halved.
3. In a large mixing bowl, toss the prepared vegetables with olive oil until they are evenly coated. This will help prevent them from sticking to the grill and add flavor.
4. Season the vegetables with salt and pepper to taste, along with any optional seasonings you like. Garlic powder, onion powder, and dried herbs add extra flavor, while a drizzle of balsamic vinegar can add sweetness and acidity.
5. Once the grill is hot, place the vegetables directly on the grill grates. You can arrange them in a single layer or use skewers for smaller vegetables to prevent them from falling through the grates.
6. Grill the vegetables for 5-10 minutes, flipping them halfway through, until they are tender and lightly charred on all sides. Cooking times will vary depending on the type and size of the vegetables, so keep an eye on them to prevent burning.
7. Once the vegetables are cooked to your liking, remove them from the grill and transfer them to a serving platter.
8. Serve the grilled vegetables hot as a delicious side dish at your BBQ.

Enjoy the smoky flavor and vibrant colors of these grilled vegetables alongside your favorite BBQ meats and other sides!

Watermelon Salad

Ingredients:

- 4 cups cubed watermelon
- 1 cup diced cucumber
- 1/2 cup crumbled vegan feta cheese
- 1/4 cup chopped fresh mint leaves
- 1/4 cup chopped fresh basil leaves
- Juice of 1 lime
- 2 tablespoons extra-virgin olive oil
- Salt and pepper to taste
- Optional: sliced red onion, balsamic glaze, chopped pistachios

Instructions:

1. In a large mixing bowl, combine the cubed watermelon, diced cucumber, crumbled vegan feta cheese, chopped fresh mint leaves, and chopped fresh basil leaves.
2. In a small bowl, whisk together the lime juice and extra-virgin olive oil to make the dressing.
3. Pour the dressing over the watermelon salad and toss everything together until well combined.
4. Season the salad with salt and pepper to taste.
5. If desired, add sliced red onion for extra flavor and crunch.
6. Transfer the watermelon salad to a serving platter or individual bowls.
7. Drizzle with balsamic glaze and sprinkle with chopped pistachios for added sweetness and crunch.
8. Serve the watermelon salad chilled as a refreshing side dish at your BBQ.

Enjoy the juicy sweetness of the watermelon combined with the freshness of the cucumber and herbs in this delicious summer salad!

Caprese Salad Skewers

Ingredients:

- Cherry tomatoes
- Fresh basil leaves
- Vegan mozzarella cheese, cubed
- Balsamic glaze (store-bought or homemade)
- Wooden skewers

Instructions:

1. Rinse the cherry tomatoes and pat them dry with a paper towel.
2. Take a wooden skewer and thread a cherry tomato onto it, followed by a folded basil leaf and a cube of vegan mozzarella cheese. Repeat this pattern until the skewer is filled, leaving a little space at the top and bottom for handling.
3. Arrange the assembled skewers on a serving platter.
4. Just before serving, drizzle the skewers with balsamic glaze for a sweet and tangy finish.
5. Serve the Caprese salad skewers immediately as a flavorful appetizer or side dish at your BBQ.

Enjoy the combination of juicy tomatoes, fresh basil, and creamy vegan mozzarella in these delightful skewers!

Fruit Salad

Ingredients:

- Assorted fresh fruits of your choice (such as strawberries, blueberries, raspberries, grapes, pineapple, kiwi, oranges, melon, etc.)
- Fresh mint leaves for garnish (optional)
- Lemon juice (optional, to prevent fruit from browning)

Instructions:

1. Wash and prepare the fruits by removing any stems, seeds, or skins as needed. Cut larger fruits like pineapple, melon, and kiwi into bite-sized pieces.
2. Place the prepared fruits in a large mixing bowl.
3. If desired, squeeze fresh lemon juice over the fruit to prevent it from browning. Toss gently to coat.
4. Arrange the mixed fruits on a serving platter or in a large bowl.
5. Garnish the fruit salad with fresh mint leaves for an extra burst of flavor and presentation (optional).
6. Serve the fruit salad immediately as a refreshing side dish or dessert at your BBQ.

Enjoy the vibrant colors and natural sweetness of this delicious fruit salad!

Deviled Eggs

Ingredients:

- 6 large eggs
- 1/4 cup vegan mayonnaise
- 1 teaspoon Dijon mustard
- 1 teaspoon apple cider vinegar
- Salt and pepper to taste
- Paprika for garnish
- Optional: chopped fresh chives or parsley for garnish

Instructions:

1. Place the eggs in a single layer in a saucepan and cover them with water. Bring the water to a boil over high heat.
2. Once the water is boiling, reduce the heat to low and let the eggs simmer for 10 minutes.
3. After 10 minutes, remove the saucepan from the heat and transfer the eggs to a bowl of ice water to cool completely.
4. Once the eggs are cooled, carefully peel them and slice them in half lengthwise. Remove the yolks and place them in a separate bowl.
5. Mash the egg yolks with a fork until they are smooth and crumbly.
6. Add the vegan mayonnaise, Dijon mustard, apple cider vinegar, salt, and pepper to the mashed egg yolks. Stir until everything is well combined and creamy.
7. Spoon the yolk mixture into the hollowed-out egg whites, dividing it evenly among them.
8. Sprinkle paprika over the filled eggs for garnish. You can also garnish with chopped fresh chives or parsley if desired.
9. Refrigerate the deviled eggs for at least 30 minutes before serving to allow the flavors to meld together.
10. Serve the deviled eggs cold as a delicious appetizer at your BBQ.

Enjoy the creamy and flavorful goodness of these classic deviled eggs!

BBQ Baked Potatoes

Ingredients:

- Russet potatoes (1 per person)
- Olive oil
- Salt
- Toppings of your choice (such as vegan butter, vegan sour cream, chopped chives, vegan bacon bits, shredded vegan cheese)

Instructions:

1. Preheat your grill to medium-high heat.
2. Wash the potatoes thoroughly and pat them dry with a paper towel.
3. Prick each potato several times with a fork to allow steam to escape during cooking.
4. Rub each potato with olive oil and sprinkle with salt.
5. Wrap each potato individually in aluminum foil.
6. Place the wrapped potatoes directly on the grill grates.
7. Close the grill lid and cook the potatoes for 45 minutes to 1 hour, or until they are tender when pierced with a fork.
8. Carefully remove the potatoes from the grill and let them cool for a few minutes.
9. Unwrap the potatoes and slice them open lengthwise.
10. Fluff the insides of the potatoes with a fork and add your desired toppings, such as vegan butter, vegan sour cream, chopped chives, vegan bacon bits, and shredded vegan cheese.
11. Serve the BBQ baked potatoes hot as a delicious side dish at your BBQ.

Enjoy the smoky flavor and fluffy texture of these BBQ baked potatoes, topped with your favorite vegan toppings!

Garlic Bread

Ingredients:

- 1 loaf of French or Italian bread
- 1/2 cup vegan butter, softened
- 4 cloves garlic, minced
- 2 tablespoons chopped fresh parsley (optional)
- Salt to taste

Instructions:

1. Preheat your oven to 375°F (190°C).
2. Slice the loaf of bread in half horizontally to create two long pieces.
3. In a small mixing bowl, combine the softened vegan butter, minced garlic, chopped fresh parsley (if using), and salt to taste. Mix until well combined.
4. Spread the garlic butter mixture evenly over the cut sides of the bread.
5. Place the bread halves on a baking sheet, cut side up.
6. Bake in the preheated oven for 10-15 minutes, or until the bread is golden brown and crispy on the edges.
7. Remove the garlic bread from the oven and let it cool for a few minutes before slicing.
8. Slice the garlic bread into individual portions and serve warm as a delicious side dish at your BBQ.

Enjoy the buttery, garlicky goodness of this classic garlic bread alongside your favorite BBQ meats and sides!

Grilled Asparagus

Ingredients:

- 1 bunch of asparagus
- 2 tablespoons olive oil
- Salt and pepper to taste
- Lemon wedges for serving (optional)

Instructions:

1. Preheat your grill to medium-high heat.
2. Wash the asparagus and trim off the tough ends. If the spears are thick, you can peel the bottom half of each spear with a vegetable peeler for tenderness.
3. Place the trimmed asparagus spears in a large mixing bowl and drizzle with olive oil. Toss to coat evenly.
4. Season the asparagus with salt and pepper to taste, ensuring they are well seasoned.
5. Arrange the asparagus spears in a single layer on the preheated grill.
6. Grill the asparagus for 5-7 minutes, turning occasionally, until they are tender and slightly charred. The cooking time may vary depending on the thickness of the asparagus spears.
7. Once the asparagus is cooked to your liking, remove them from the grill and transfer them to a serving platter.
8. Serve the grilled asparagus hot, optionally with lemon wedges for squeezing over the top.

Enjoy the delicious smoky flavor and tender texture of grilled asparagus as a delightful side dish at your BBQ!

Stuffed Jalapeños

Ingredients:

- 12 fresh jalapeño peppers
- 8 oz (about 1 cup) vegan cream cheese, softened
- 1/2 cup shredded vegan cheddar cheese
- 2 cloves garlic, minced
- 1/4 teaspoon onion powder
- Salt and pepper to taste
- Optional: vegan bacon bits or chopped cilantro for garnish

Instructions:

1. Preheat your oven to 400°F (200°C). Line a baking sheet with parchment paper.
2. Wash the jalapeño peppers and slice them in half lengthwise. Remove the seeds and membranes using a spoon, being careful to avoid touching your eyes or face.
3. In a mixing bowl, combine the softened vegan cream cheese, shredded vegan cheddar cheese, minced garlic, onion powder, salt, and pepper. Mix until well combined.
4. Spoon the cheese mixture into each jalapeño half, filling them generously.
5. Place the stuffed jalapeños on the prepared baking sheet, cut side up.
6. Bake in the preheated oven for 15-20 minutes, or until the jalapeños are softened and the cheese is melted and bubbly.
7. If desired, sprinkle vegan bacon bits or chopped cilantro over the top of the stuffed jalapeños for garnish.
8. Remove the stuffed jalapeños from the oven and let them cool for a few minutes before serving.
9. Serve the stuffed jalapeños warm as a spicy and flavorful appetizer at your BBQ.

Enjoy the creamy and cheesy goodness of these stuffed jalapeños, with just the right amount of heat!

Spinach and Artichoke Dip

Ingredients:

- 1 tablespoon olive oil
- 2 cloves garlic, minced
- 1 (10 oz) package frozen chopped spinach, thawed and drained
- 1 (14 oz) can artichoke hearts, drained and chopped
- 1 (8 oz) package vegan cream cheese, softened
- 1/2 cup vegan mayonnaise
- 1/2 cup shredded vegan mozzarella cheese
- 1/4 cup nutritional yeast (optional, for extra cheesy flavor)
- Salt and pepper to taste
- Optional: crushed red pepper flakes for a bit of heat
- Optional: vegan Parmesan cheese for topping

Instructions:

1. Preheat your oven to 375°F (190°C).
2. Heat the olive oil in a skillet over medium heat. Add the minced garlic and sauté for 1-2 minutes, until fragrant.
3. Add the thawed and drained chopped spinach to the skillet and cook for 3-4 minutes, until heated through.
4. Stir in the chopped artichoke hearts and cook for an additional 2-3 minutes.
5. In a large mixing bowl, combine the softened vegan cream cheese, vegan mayonnaise, shredded vegan mozzarella cheese, and nutritional yeast (if using). Mix until well combined.
6. Add the cooked spinach and artichoke mixture to the bowl with the cheese mixture. Stir until everything is evenly combined.
7. Season the dip with salt, pepper, and crushed red pepper flakes to taste.
8. Transfer the spinach and artichoke dip to a baking dish and spread it out evenly.
9. If desired, sprinkle vegan Parmesan cheese over the top of the dip for extra flavor.
10. Bake in the preheated oven for 20-25 minutes, or until the dip is bubbly and golden brown on top.
11. Remove the dip from the oven and let it cool for a few minutes before serving.

12. Serve the spinach and artichoke dip warm with your favorite dippers, such as tortilla chips, breadsticks, or veggie sticks.

Enjoy the creamy and cheesy goodness of this classic spinach and artichoke dip at your next BBQ or gathering!

BBQ Tofu Skewers

Ingredients:

- 1 block extra-firm tofu, pressed and drained
- 1/2 cup BBQ sauce (store-bought or homemade)
- 2 tablespoons olive oil
- 1 tablespoon soy sauce or tamari
- 1 tablespoon maple syrup or agave syrup
- 1 teaspoon garlic powder
- 1 teaspoon smoked paprika
- Salt and pepper to taste
- Wooden skewers, soaked in water for 30 minutes

Instructions:

1. Preheat your grill to medium-high heat.
2. Cut the pressed and drained tofu into cubes, approximately 1 inch in size.
3. In a mixing bowl, whisk together the BBQ sauce, olive oil, soy sauce or tamari, maple syrup or agave syrup, garlic powder, smoked paprika, salt, and pepper.
4. Add the tofu cubes to the bowl with the BBQ marinade and toss gently to coat the tofu evenly. Let it marinate for at least 15 minutes, or longer if time allows.
5. Thread the marinated tofu cubes onto the soaked wooden skewers, leaving a little space between each cube.
6. Place the tofu skewers on the preheated grill and cook for 5-7 minutes on each side, or until the tofu is lightly charred and heated through, basting with any remaining marinade as needed.
7. Once the tofu skewers are cooked to your liking, remove them from the grill and transfer them to a serving platter.
8. Serve the BBQ tofu skewers hot as a delicious and flavorful plant-based option at your BBQ.

Enjoy the smoky and savory flavor of these BBQ tofu skewers, perfect for grilling season!

Cucumber Salad

Ingredients:

- 2 large cucumbers, thinly sliced
- 1/4 cup red onion, thinly sliced
- 1/4 cup fresh dill, chopped
- 2 tablespoons apple cider vinegar
- 1 tablespoon olive oil
- 1 teaspoon sugar or maple syrup
- Salt and pepper to taste

Instructions:

1. In a large mixing bowl, combine the thinly sliced cucumbers, red onion, and chopped fresh dill.
2. In a small bowl, whisk together the apple cider vinegar, olive oil, sugar or maple syrup, salt, and pepper until well combined.
3. Pour the dressing over the cucumber mixture and toss until everything is evenly coated.
4. Cover the bowl and refrigerate the cucumber salad for at least 30 minutes to allow the flavors to meld together.
5. Before serving, give the cucumber salad a final toss and adjust the seasoning if needed.
6. Serve the cucumber salad cold as a refreshing side dish at your BBQ.

Enjoy the crisp and tangy flavor of this delicious cucumber salad alongside your favorite BBQ meats and sides!

Grilled Pineapple

Ingredients:

- 1 ripe pineapple
- 2 tablespoons brown sugar (optional)
- 1 teaspoon ground cinnamon (optional)
- Wooden skewers, soaked in water for 30 minutes (optional)

Instructions:

1. Preheat your grill to medium-high heat.
2. Peel the pineapple and remove the eyes. Slice the pineapple into rounds or wedges, about 1/2 to 1 inch thick.
3. If desired, sprinkle both sides of the pineapple slices with brown sugar and ground cinnamon for extra sweetness and flavor.
4. Thread the pineapple slices onto the soaked wooden skewers, if using, or place them directly on the grill grates.
5. Grill the pineapple slices for 2-3 minutes on each side, or until they are lightly charred and caramelized.
6. Once the pineapple slices are grilled to your liking, remove them from the grill and transfer them to a serving platter.
7. Serve the grilled pineapple slices hot as a delicious and refreshing dessert or side dish at your BBQ.

Enjoy the juicy sweetness and smoky flavor of grilled pineapple as a delightful treat at your next BBQ gathering!

Roasted Sweet Potatoes

Ingredients:

- 2 large sweet potatoes, peeled and cut into 1-inch cubes
- 2 tablespoons olive oil
- 1 teaspoon smoked paprika
- 1 teaspoon garlic powder
- 1/2 teaspoon ground cumin
- Salt and pepper to taste
- Optional: chopped fresh parsley or cilantro for garnish

Instructions:

1. Preheat your oven to 400°F (200°C) and line a baking sheet with parchment paper or aluminum foil.
2. In a large mixing bowl, toss the sweet potato cubes with olive oil, smoked paprika, garlic powder, ground cumin, salt, and pepper until evenly coated.
3. Spread the seasoned sweet potato cubes in a single layer on the prepared baking sheet.
4. Roast the sweet potatoes in the preheated oven for 25-30 minutes, flipping halfway through, or until they are tender and caramelized on the edges.
5. Once the sweet potatoes are roasted to your liking, remove them from the oven and transfer them to a serving dish.
6. If desired, garnish the roasted sweet potatoes with chopped fresh parsley or cilantro for added freshness and color.
7. Serve the roasted sweet potatoes hot as a delicious and flavorful side dish at your BBQ.

Enjoy the tender and caramelized goodness of these roasted sweet potatoes alongside your favorite BBQ meats and sides!

BBQ Brussels Sprouts

Ingredients:

- 1 lb Brussels sprouts, trimmed and halved
- 2 tablespoons olive oil
- 2 tablespoons BBQ sauce (store-bought or homemade)
- 1 tablespoon maple syrup or agave syrup
- 1 teaspoon smoked paprika
- 1/2 teaspoon garlic powder
- Salt and pepper to taste

Instructions:

1. Preheat your grill to medium-high heat.
2. In a large mixing bowl, toss the Brussels sprout halves with olive oil until evenly coated.
3. In a small bowl, whisk together the BBQ sauce, maple syrup or agave syrup, smoked paprika, garlic powder, salt, and pepper to make the BBQ marinade.
4. Pour the BBQ marinade over the Brussels sprouts and toss until they are evenly coated.
5. Thread the Brussels sprout halves onto skewers, if desired, or place them directly on the grill grates.
6. Grill the Brussels sprouts for 10-15 minutes, turning occasionally, until they are tender and charred on the edges.
7. Once the Brussels sprouts are cooked to your liking, remove them from the grill and transfer them to a serving platter.
8. Serve the BBQ Brussels sprouts hot as a flavorful and nutritious side dish at your BBQ.

Enjoy the smoky and tangy flavor of these BBQ Brussels sprouts alongside your favorite BBQ meats and other sides!

Vegan Coleslaw

Ingredients:

- 1/2 head of green cabbage, thinly sliced
- 1/2 head of purple cabbage, thinly sliced
- 2 large carrots, grated
- 1/2 cup vegan mayonnaise
- 2 tablespoons apple cider vinegar
- 1 tablespoon Dijon mustard
- 1 tablespoon maple syrup or agave syrup
- 1 teaspoon celery seeds (optional)
- Salt and pepper to taste

Instructions:

1. In a large mixing bowl, combine the thinly sliced green cabbage, purple cabbage, and grated carrots.
2. In a separate small bowl, whisk together the vegan mayonnaise, apple cider vinegar, Dijon mustard, maple syrup or agave syrup, and celery seeds (if using) until well combined.
3. Pour the dressing over the cabbage and carrot mixture and toss until everything is evenly coated.
4. Season the coleslaw with salt and pepper to taste, adjusting as needed.
5. Cover the bowl and refrigerate the coleslaw for at least 30 minutes to allow the flavors to meld together.
6. Before serving, give the coleslaw a final toss to redistribute the dressing.
7. Serve the vegan coleslaw cold as a creamy and crunchy side dish at your BBQ.

Enjoy the fresh and tangy flavors of this delicious vegan coleslaw alongside your favorite BBQ meats and other sides!

Grilled Peaches with Balsamic Glaze

Ingredients:

- 4 ripe peaches, halved and pitted
- 2 tablespoons olive oil
- 2 tablespoons brown sugar
- 1/4 teaspoon ground cinnamon
- Pinch of salt
- Balsamic glaze (store-bought or homemade)
- Optional toppings: chopped fresh mint, vegan vanilla ice cream

Instructions:

1. Preheat your grill to medium-high heat.
2. In a small bowl, whisk together the olive oil, brown sugar, ground cinnamon, and a pinch of salt until well combined.
3. Brush the cut side of each peach half with the olive oil mixture.
4. Place the peaches cut side down on the preheated grill.
5. Grill the peaches for 3-4 minutes, or until they have grill marks and are caramelized.
6. Carefully flip the peaches with tongs and grill for an additional 2-3 minutes on the other side.
7. Once the peaches are grilled to your liking, remove them from the grill and transfer them to a serving platter.
8. Drizzle the grilled peaches with balsamic glaze.
9. If desired, sprinkle chopped fresh mint over the top of the peaches for added freshness.
10. Serve the grilled peaches warm as a delicious and elegant dessert at your BBQ. Optionally, serve with a scoop of vegan vanilla ice cream for an extra indulgent treat.

Enjoy the sweet and smoky flavor of these grilled peaches with balsamic glaze as a delightful finale to your BBQ meal!

Antipasto Platter

Ingredients:

- Assorted cured meats (such as prosciutto, salami, and pepperoni)
- Assorted cheeses (such as mozzarella, provolone, and gouda)
- Marinated olives (such as kalamata and green olives)
- Roasted vegetables (such as cherry tomatoes, bell peppers, and artichoke hearts)
- Marinated vegetables (such as roasted red peppers and marinated mushrooms)
- Pickled vegetables (such as pickled onions and cornichons)
- Breadsticks or crostini
- Crackers
- Nuts (such as almonds or walnuts)
- Fresh herbs for garnish (such as basil or parsley)
- Optional: dips or spreads (such as hummus or tapenade)
- Optional: fresh fruits (such as grapes or figs)

Instructions:

1. Start by arranging a large platter or board that will accommodate all the ingredients.
2. Begin by placing the cured meats on the platter, folding or rolling them for an attractive presentation.
3. Next, arrange the assorted cheeses around the cured meats, leaving space for other ingredients.
4. Fill in the gaps with marinated olives, roasted vegetables, marinated vegetables, and pickled vegetables.
5. Add breadsticks or crostini to the platter, arranging them in a decorative pattern.
6. Scatter nuts around the platter for added texture and flavor.
7. Garnish the platter with fresh herbs for a pop of color and freshness.
8. Optionally, serve dips or spreads in small bowls alongside the platter for dipping.
9. Optionally, add fresh fruits to the platter for a sweet contrast to the savory flavors.
10. Serve the antipasto platter as a delicious appetizer or side dish at your BBQ.

Enjoy the variety of flavors and textures on your antipasto platter as a delightful addition to your BBQ spread!

Hawaiian Macaroni Salad

Ingredients:

- 1 lb elbow macaroni
- 1 cup vegan mayonnaise
- 1/4 cup apple cider vinegar
- 1 tablespoon granulated sugar
- 1/2 teaspoon garlic powder
- 1/2 teaspoon onion powder
- Salt and pepper to taste
- 2 medium carrots, grated
- 1/2 cup chopped celery
- 1/4 cup chopped green onions

Instructions:

1. Cook the elbow macaroni according to the package instructions until al dente. Drain and rinse the cooked macaroni under cold water to cool it down.
2. In a large mixing bowl, whisk together the vegan mayonnaise, apple cider vinegar, granulated sugar, garlic powder, onion powder, salt, and pepper until smooth and well combined.
3. Add the cooked and cooled macaroni to the bowl with the dressing, along with the grated carrots, chopped celery, and chopped green onions.
4. Toss everything together until the macaroni and vegetables are evenly coated with the dressing.
5. Cover the bowl and refrigerate the Hawaiian macaroni salad for at least 1 hour, or until chilled.
6. Before serving, give the macaroni salad a final toss and adjust the seasoning if needed.
7. Serve the Hawaiian macaroni salad cold as a creamy and flavorful side dish at your BBQ.

Enjoy the creamy texture and tangy flavor of this Hawaiian-style macaroni salad alongside your favorite BBQ meats and sides!

Grilled Zucchini

Ingredients:

- 2 medium zucchini
- 2 tablespoons olive oil
- Salt and pepper to taste
- Optional seasonings: garlic powder, onion powder, dried herbs (such as thyme or oregano), chili flakes

Instructions:

1. Preheat your grill to medium-high heat.
2. Wash the zucchini and trim off the ends. Cut the zucchini lengthwise into slices, about 1/4 to 1/2 inch thick.
3. Place the zucchini slices in a large mixing bowl. Drizzle olive oil over the zucchini and toss to coat evenly.
4. Season the zucchini slices with salt and pepper to taste, along with any optional seasonings you like, such as garlic powder, onion powder, dried herbs, or chili flakes.
5. Once the grill is hot, place the zucchini slices directly on the grill grates.
6. Grill the zucchini slices for 3-4 minutes on each side, or until they are tender and lightly charred.
7. Once the zucchini slices are grilled to your liking, remove them from the grill and transfer them to a serving platter.
8. Serve the grilled zucchini slices hot as a delicious and healthy side dish at your BBQ.

Enjoy the smoky flavor and tender texture of grilled zucchini alongside your favorite BBQ meats and other sides!

Southern Hush Puppies

Ingredients:

- 1 cup cornmeal
- 1/2 cup all-purpose flour
- 1 teaspoon baking powder
- 1/2 teaspoon baking soda
- 1/2 teaspoon salt
- 1/2 teaspoon garlic powder
- 1/2 teaspoon onion powder
- 1/4 teaspoon paprika
- 1/4 teaspoon black pepper
- 1/2 cup finely chopped onion
- 1/4 cup finely chopped green bell pepper
- 1/4 cup finely chopped celery
- 1/2 cup canned creamed corn
- 1/4 cup unsweetened plant-based milk
- 1 tablespoon hot sauce (optional)
- Vegetable oil, for frying

Instructions:

1. In a large mixing bowl, whisk together the cornmeal, flour, baking powder, baking soda, salt, garlic powder, onion powder, paprika, and black pepper.
2. Stir in the finely chopped onion, green bell pepper, and celery until evenly distributed.
3. In a separate small bowl, mix together the canned creamed corn, plant-based milk, and hot sauce (if using).
4. Pour the wet ingredients into the dry ingredients and stir until just combined. Be careful not to overmix.
5. Heat vegetable oil in a deep fryer or large skillet to 350°F (175°C).
6. Drop spoonfuls of the batter into the hot oil, frying in batches to avoid overcrowding.
7. Fry the hush puppies for 2-3 minutes, or until they are golden brown and cooked through, flipping them halfway through cooking.

8. Use a slotted spoon to transfer the hush puppies to a paper towel-lined plate to drain excess oil.
9. Serve the hush puppies hot as a delicious and crispy side dish at your BBQ.

Enjoy the crispy exterior and tender interior of these classic Southern hush puppies!

BBQ Cauliflower Wings

Ingredients:

For the cauliflower wings:

- 1 head cauliflower, cut into florets
- 1 cup all-purpose flour (or chickpea flour for a gluten-free option)
- 1 cup plant-based milk (such as almond milk or soy milk)
- 1 teaspoon garlic powder
- 1 teaspoon onion powder
- 1/2 teaspoon paprika
- Salt and pepper to taste

For the BBQ sauce:

- 1/2 cup barbecue sauce (store-bought or homemade)
- 2 tablespoons maple syrup or agave syrup
- 1 tablespoon soy sauce or tamari
- 1 tablespoon apple cider vinegar
- 1 teaspoon garlic powder
- 1/2 teaspoon smoked paprika

Instructions:

1. Preheat your oven to 450°F (230°C) and line a baking sheet with parchment paper.
2. In a large mixing bowl, whisk together the flour, plant-based milk, garlic powder, onion powder, paprika, salt, and pepper until smooth and well combined.
3. Dip each cauliflower floret into the batter, coating it evenly, and shake off any excess batter.
4. Place the battered cauliflower florets in a single layer on the prepared baking sheet.
5. Bake in the preheated oven for 20-25 minutes, or until the cauliflower is golden brown and crispy.

6. While the cauliflower is baking, prepare the BBQ sauce. In a small saucepan, combine the barbecue sauce, maple syrup or agave syrup, soy sauce or tamari, apple cider vinegar, garlic powder, and smoked paprika. Cook over medium heat for 5-7 minutes, stirring occasionally, until the sauce is heated through and slightly thickened.
7. Once the cauliflower is done baking, remove it from the oven and transfer it to a large mixing bowl.
8. Pour the BBQ sauce over the baked cauliflower and toss until the cauliflower is evenly coated with the sauce.
9. Return the cauliflower to the baking sheet and bake for an additional 5-7 minutes, or until the sauce is caramelized and sticky.
10. Remove the BBQ cauliflower wings from the oven and let them cool for a few minutes before serving.
11. Serve the BBQ cauliflower wings hot as a delicious and flavorful appetizer or side dish at your BBQ.

Enjoy the crispy texture and bold flavor of these BBQ cauliflower wings!

Tomato and Mozzarella Salad

Ingredients:

- 3-4 ripe tomatoes, sliced
- 8 oz (about 1 cup) fresh mozzarella cheese, sliced
- Fresh basil leaves
- Extra virgin olive oil
- Balsamic glaze (store-bought or homemade)
- Salt and pepper to taste

Instructions:

1. Arrange the sliced tomatoes and fresh mozzarella cheese on a serving platter, alternating them in a single layer.
2. Tuck fresh basil leaves in between the tomato and mozzarella slices for added flavor and freshness.
3. Drizzle extra virgin olive oil over the tomato and mozzarella slices, ensuring they are evenly coated.
4. Drizzle balsamic glaze over the top of the salad for a sweet and tangy flavor contrast.
5. Season the salad with salt and pepper to taste.
6. Optionally, garnish the salad with additional fresh basil leaves for presentation.
7. Serve the tomato and mozzarella salad immediately as a light and refreshing appetizer or side dish at your BBQ.

Enjoy the vibrant colors and delicious flavors of this classic tomato and mozzarella salad!

Grilled Eggplant

Ingredients:

- 1 large eggplant
- 2-3 tablespoons olive oil
- Salt and pepper to taste
- Optional: minced garlic, dried herbs (such as oregano or thyme), red pepper flakes

Instructions:

1. Preheat your grill to medium-high heat.
2. Wash the eggplant and trim off the ends. Slice the eggplant into rounds, about 1/2 inch thick.
3. Place the eggplant slices in a single layer on a baking sheet or large plate. Brush both sides of the eggplant slices with olive oil.
4. Season the eggplant slices with salt and pepper to taste, along with any optional seasonings you like, such as minced garlic, dried herbs, or red pepper flakes.
5. Once the grill is hot, place the eggplant slices directly on the grill grates.
6. Grill the eggplant slices for 3-4 minutes on each side, or until they are tender and have grill marks.
7. Once the eggplant slices are grilled to your liking, remove them from the grill and transfer them to a serving platter.
8. Serve the grilled eggplant slices hot as a delicious and flavorful side dish at your BBQ.

Enjoy the smoky flavor and tender texture of grilled eggplant alongside your favorite BBQ meats and other sides!

Cowboy Caviar (Black Bean Salad)

Ingredients:

- 1 (15 oz) can black beans, drained and rinsed
- 1 (15 oz) can black-eyed peas, drained and rinsed
- 1 cup corn kernels (fresh, canned, or thawed if frozen)
- 1 red bell pepper, diced
- 1 green bell pepper, diced
- 1 jalapeño pepper, seeded and minced
- 1/2 red onion, diced
- 2 cloves garlic, minced
- 1/4 cup chopped fresh cilantro
- Juice of 2 limes
- 2 tablespoons olive oil
- 1 tablespoon apple cider vinegar
- 1 teaspoon ground cumin
- 1/2 teaspoon chili powder
- Salt and pepper to taste
- Optional: diced avocado for garnish

Instructions:

1. In a large mixing bowl, combine the black beans, black-eyed peas, corn kernels, diced red bell pepper, diced green bell pepper, minced jalapeño pepper, diced red onion, minced garlic, and chopped fresh cilantro.
2. In a small bowl, whisk together the lime juice, olive oil, apple cider vinegar, ground cumin, chili powder, salt, and pepper until well combined.
3. Pour the dressing over the black bean mixture and toss until everything is evenly coated.
4. Cover the bowl and refrigerate the cowboy caviar for at least 30 minutes to allow the flavors to meld together.
5. Before serving, give the cowboy caviar a final toss and adjust the seasoning if needed.
6. Optionally, garnish the cowboy caviar with diced avocado for added creaminess and flavor.

7. Serve the cowboy caviar chilled as a delicious and colorful side dish or appetizer at your BBQ.

Enjoy the fresh and vibrant flavors of this cowboy caviar alongside your favorite BBQ meats and other sides!

Grilled Portobello Mushrooms

Ingredients:

- 4 large portobello mushrooms
- 2 tablespoons balsamic vinegar
- 2 tablespoons soy sauce or tamari
- 2 cloves garlic, minced
- 2 tablespoons olive oil
- Salt and pepper to taste
- Optional: chopped fresh herbs (such as parsley or thyme) for garnish

Instructions:

1. Clean the portobello mushrooms by gently wiping them with a damp cloth or paper towel to remove any dirt. Remove the stems and discard them.
2. In a shallow dish or large resealable plastic bag, whisk together the balsamic vinegar, soy sauce or tamari, minced garlic, and olive oil to make the marinade.
3. Place the cleaned portobello mushrooms in the marinade, turning them to coat evenly. Allow them to marinate for at least 30 minutes, or up to 2 hours in the refrigerator.
4. Preheat your grill to medium-high heat.
5. Remove the marinated portobello mushrooms from the marinade and shake off any excess liquid. Season them with salt and pepper to taste.
6. Place the portobello mushrooms on the preheated grill, gill side down. Grill for 4-5 minutes on each side, or until they are tender and grill marks appear.
7. Once the portobello mushrooms are grilled to your liking, remove them from the grill and transfer them to a serving platter.
8. Optionally, garnish the grilled portobello mushrooms with chopped fresh herbs for added flavor and freshness.
9. Serve the grilled portobello mushrooms hot as a delicious and savory side dish or main course at your BBQ.

Enjoy the meaty texture and rich flavor of these grilled portobello mushrooms!

BBQ Cornbread Muffins

Ingredients:

- 1 cup cornmeal
- 1 cup all-purpose flour
- 1 tablespoon baking powder
- 1/2 teaspoon baking soda
- 1/2 teaspoon salt
- 1/4 cup granulated sugar
- 1 cup plant-based milk (such as almond milk or soy milk)
- 1/4 cup vegetable oil
- 1/4 cup barbecue sauce
- 1 tablespoon apple cider vinegar
- 1/2 cup corn kernels (fresh, canned, or thawed if frozen)
- Optional: chopped green onions or jalapeños for added flavor

Instructions:

1. Preheat your oven to 375°F (190°C). Line a muffin tin with paper liners or lightly grease the muffin cups.
2. In a large mixing bowl, whisk together the cornmeal, all-purpose flour, baking powder, baking soda, salt, and granulated sugar until well combined.
3. In a separate small bowl, mix together the plant-based milk, vegetable oil, barbecue sauce, and apple cider vinegar until smooth.
4. Pour the wet ingredients into the dry ingredients and stir until just combined. Be careful not to overmix.
5. Gently fold in the corn kernels and chopped green onions or jalapeños, if using.
6. Spoon the batter into the prepared muffin cups, filling each cup about 3/4 full.
7. Bake in the preheated oven for 15-20 minutes, or until the muffins are golden brown and a toothpick inserted into the center comes out clean.
8. Remove the muffins from the oven and let them cool in the muffin tin for a few minutes before transferring them to a wire rack to cool completely.
9. Serve the BBQ cornbread muffins warm as a delicious and savory side dish at your BBQ.

Enjoy the smoky flavor and tender texture of these BBQ cornbread muffins alongside your favorite BBQ meats and other sides!

Broccoli Salad

Ingredients:

- 4 cups broccoli florets, chopped into bite-sized pieces
- 1/2 cup red onion, finely chopped
- 1/2 cup dried cranberries or raisins
- 1/2 cup sunflower seeds or chopped almonds
- 1/2 cup vegan mayonnaise
- 2 tablespoons apple cider vinegar
- 1 tablespoon maple syrup or agave syrup
- Salt and pepper to taste

Instructions:

1. In a large mixing bowl, combine the chopped broccoli florets, finely chopped red onion, dried cranberries or raisins, and sunflower seeds or chopped almonds.
2. In a separate small bowl, whisk together the vegan mayonnaise, apple cider vinegar, maple syrup or agave syrup, salt, and pepper until well combined.
3. Pour the dressing over the broccoli mixture and toss until everything is evenly coated.
4. Cover the bowl and refrigerate the broccoli salad for at least 1 hour, or until chilled.
5. Before serving, give the broccoli salad a final toss and adjust the seasoning if needed.
6. Serve the broccoli salad cold as a delicious and nutritious side dish at your BBQ.

Enjoy the fresh and vibrant flavors of this broccoli salad alongside your favorite BBQ meats and other sides!

Grilled Romaine Lettuce

Ingredients:

- 2 heads of romaine lettuce, halved lengthwise
- Olive oil
- Salt and pepper to taste
- Optional: Balsamic glaze, shaved Parmesan cheese, cherry tomatoes, croutons

Instructions:

1. Preheat your grill to medium-high heat.
2. Brush the cut side of each romaine lettuce half with olive oil, ensuring they are evenly coated. Season with salt and pepper to taste.
3. Place the romaine lettuce halves cut side down on the preheated grill.
4. Grill the romaine lettuce for 1-2 minutes, or until grill marks appear and the lettuce begins to wilt slightly.
5. Carefully flip the romaine lettuce halves with tongs and grill for an additional 1-2 minutes on the other side.
6. Once the romaine lettuce is lightly charred and slightly wilted, remove them from the grill and transfer them to a serving platter.
7. Optionally, drizzle the grilled romaine lettuce with balsamic glaze and sprinkle with shaved Parmesan cheese.
8. Serve the grilled romaine lettuce immediately as a delicious and unique salad base at your BBQ. Optionally, add cherry tomatoes and croutons for extra flavor and texture.

Enjoy the smoky flavor and crisp texture of grilled romaine lettuce as a delightful addition to your BBQ spread!

Mediterranean Orzo Salad

Ingredients:

- 1 1/2 cups uncooked orzo pasta
- 1 pint cherry tomatoes, halved
- 1 cucumber, diced
- 1/2 red onion, finely chopped
- 1/2 cup Kalamata olives, pitted and halved
- 1/2 cup crumbled feta cheese (optional, omit for vegan version)
- 1/4 cup chopped fresh parsley
- 1/4 cup chopped fresh basil
- 1/4 cup extra virgin olive oil
- 2 tablespoons red wine vinegar
- 1 clove garlic, minced
- Salt and pepper to taste
- Optional: Lemon zest, chopped fresh oregano, chopped fresh mint

Instructions:

1. Cook the orzo pasta according to the package instructions until al dente. Drain and rinse the cooked orzo under cold water to cool it down.
2. In a large mixing bowl, combine the cooked orzo pasta, cherry tomatoes, diced cucumber, finely chopped red onion, halved Kalamata olives, crumbled feta cheese (if using), chopped fresh parsley, and chopped fresh basil.
3. In a small bowl, whisk together the extra virgin olive oil, red wine vinegar, minced garlic, salt, and pepper until well combined.
4. Pour the dressing over the orzo salad and toss until everything is evenly coated.
5. Taste the salad and adjust the seasoning if needed. You can also add lemon zest, chopped fresh oregano, or chopped fresh mint for extra flavor if desired.
6. Cover the bowl and refrigerate the Mediterranean orzo salad for at least 1 hour, or until chilled.
7. Before serving, give the salad a final toss to redistribute the dressing and ingredients.
8. Serve the Mediterranean orzo salad cold as a delicious and refreshing side dish at your BBQ.

Enjoy the vibrant flavors and textures of this Mediterranean-inspired orzo salad alongside your favorite BBQ meats and other sides!

BBQ Potato Wedges

Ingredients:

- 4 large potatoes (such as Russet or Yukon Gold), scrubbed and cut into wedges
- 2 tablespoons olive oil
- 1 teaspoon garlic powder
- 1 teaspoon onion powder
- 1 teaspoon paprika
- 1/2 teaspoon chili powder
- 1/2 teaspoon dried oregano
- Salt and pepper to taste
- BBQ sauce for serving

Instructions:

1. Preheat your oven to 425°F (220°C). Line a baking sheet with parchment paper or aluminum foil for easy cleanup.
2. In a large mixing bowl, toss the potato wedges with olive oil until evenly coated.
3. In a small bowl, mix together the garlic powder, onion powder, paprika, chili powder, dried oregano, salt, and pepper.
4. Sprinkle the seasoning mixture over the potato wedges and toss until they are evenly coated with the spices.
5. Arrange the seasoned potato wedges in a single layer on the prepared baking sheet, making sure they are not overcrowded.
6. Bake the potato wedges in the preheated oven for 25-30 minutes, flipping halfway through cooking, or until they are golden brown and crispy on the outside and tender on the inside.
7. Once the potato wedges are done baking, remove them from the oven and transfer them to a serving platter.
8. Serve the BBQ potato wedges hot with your favorite BBQ sauce for dipping.

Enjoy the smoky flavor and crispy texture of these BBQ potato wedges as a delicious side dish at your BBQ!

Stuffed Mushrooms

Ingredients:

- 12 large mushrooms, stems removed and cleaned
- 1 tablespoon olive oil
- 1 small onion, finely chopped
- 2 cloves garlic, minced
- 1/2 cup breadcrumbs
- 1/4 cup grated Parmesan cheese (optional, omit for vegan version)
- 2 tablespoons chopped fresh parsley
- Salt and pepper to taste
- Optional: 1/4 cup chopped sun-dried tomatoes, 1/4 cup chopped spinach, 1/4 cup chopped roasted red peppers

Instructions:

1. Preheat your oven to 375°F (190°C). Line a baking sheet with parchment paper or aluminum foil for easy cleanup.
2. Remove the stems from the mushrooms and set them aside. Place the mushroom caps on the prepared baking sheet.
3. Finely chop the mushroom stems.
4. In a skillet, heat olive oil over medium heat. Add the chopped onion and cook until softened, about 3-4 minutes.
5. Add the minced garlic and chopped mushroom stems to the skillet. Cook for an additional 2-3 minutes, or until the mushrooms are tender and any excess moisture has evaporated.
6. Remove the skillet from the heat and stir in the breadcrumbs, grated Parmesan cheese (if using), chopped fresh parsley, salt, and pepper. If desired, add chopped sun-dried tomatoes, chopped spinach, or chopped roasted red peppers for extra flavor.
7. Spoon the filling mixture into each mushroom cap, pressing down gently to pack the filling.
8. Bake the stuffed mushrooms in the preheated oven for 15-20 minutes, or until the mushrooms are tender and the filling is golden brown and crispy.
9. Once the stuffed mushrooms are done baking, remove them from the oven and let them cool for a few minutes before serving.

10. Serve the stuffed mushrooms warm as a delicious appetizer or side dish at your BBQ.

Enjoy the savory flavor and hearty texture of these stuffed mushrooms!

Three Bean Salad

Ingredients:

- 1 can (15 ounces) kidney beans, drained and rinsed
- 1 can (15 ounces) cannellini beans, drained and rinsed
- 1 can (15 ounces) chickpeas (garbanzo beans), drained and rinsed
- 1/2 red onion, finely chopped
- 1/2 green bell pepper, finely chopped
- 1/2 cup chopped fresh parsley
- 1/4 cup olive oil
- 1/4 cup apple cider vinegar
- 2 tablespoons granulated sugar
- 1 teaspoon Dijon mustard
- Salt and pepper to taste

Instructions:

1. In a large mixing bowl, combine the kidney beans, cannellini beans, chickpeas, finely chopped red onion, finely chopped green bell pepper, and chopped fresh parsley.
2. In a small bowl, whisk together the olive oil, apple cider vinegar, granulated sugar, Dijon mustard, salt, and pepper until well combined.
3. Pour the dressing over the bean mixture and toss until everything is evenly coated.
4. Cover the bowl and refrigerate the three bean salad for at least 1 hour, or until chilled.
5. Before serving, give the salad a final toss to redistribute the dressing and ingredients.
6. Serve the three bean salad cold as a delicious and nutritious side dish at your BBQ.

Enjoy the combination of flavors and textures in this classic three bean salad!

Grilled Bell Pepper Salad

Ingredients:

- 3-4 bell peppers (assorted colors), halved and seeded
- 2 tablespoons olive oil
- 1 tablespoon balsamic vinegar
- 2 cloves garlic, minced
- 1 teaspoon dried Italian herbs (such as oregano, basil, and thyme)
- Salt and pepper to taste
- Optional: chopped fresh parsley or basil for garnish

Instructions:

1. Preheat your grill to medium-high heat.
2. In a small bowl, whisk together the olive oil, balsamic vinegar, minced garlic, dried Italian herbs, salt, and pepper to make the marinade.
3. Place the halved bell peppers in a shallow dish or large resealable plastic bag. Pour the marinade over the bell peppers, turning them to coat evenly. Let them marinate for at least 15-20 minutes.
4. Once the grill is hot, place the marinated bell peppers on the grill, cut side down.
5. Grill the bell peppers for 4-5 minutes on each side, or until they are charred and tender.
6. Remove the grilled bell peppers from the grill and let them cool slightly.
7. Once the bell peppers are cool enough to handle, slice them into strips or bite-sized pieces.
8. Place the grilled bell pepper strips in a serving bowl and drizzle any remaining marinade over the top.
9. Optionally, garnish the grilled bell pepper salad with chopped fresh parsley or basil for added freshness.
10. Serve the grilled bell pepper salad warm or at room temperature as a delicious and vibrant side dish at your BBQ.

Enjoy the smoky flavor and vibrant colors of this grilled bell pepper salad alongside your favorite BBQ meats and other sides!

Corn and Avocado Salad

Ingredients:

- 2 cups corn kernels (fresh, canned, or thawed if frozen)
- 2 ripe avocados, diced
- 1/2 cup cherry tomatoes, halved
- 1/4 cup red onion, finely chopped
- 1/4 cup chopped fresh cilantro
- Juice of 1 lime
- 2 tablespoons extra virgin olive oil
- Salt and pepper to taste

Instructions:

1. In a large mixing bowl, combine the corn kernels, diced avocado, halved cherry tomatoes, finely chopped red onion, and chopped fresh cilantro.
2. In a small bowl, whisk together the lime juice, extra virgin olive oil, salt, and pepper until well combined.
3. Pour the dressing over the corn and avocado mixture and toss until everything is evenly coated.
4. Taste the salad and adjust the seasoning if needed.
5. Cover the bowl and refrigerate the corn and avocado salad for at least 30 minutes to allow the flavors to meld together.
6. Before serving, give the salad a final toss to redistribute the dressing and ingredients.
7. Serve the corn and avocado salad cold as a delicious and creamy side dish at your BBQ.

Enjoy the fresh and vibrant flavors of this corn and avocado salad alongside your favorite BBQ meats and other sides!

BBQ Green Beans

Ingredients:

- 1 pound fresh green beans, trimmed
- 2 tablespoons olive oil
- 2 cloves garlic, minced
- 1/4 cup barbecue sauce
- Salt and pepper to taste
- Optional: crushed red pepper flakes for heat, sliced almonds or chopped bacon for added texture

Instructions:

1. Preheat your grill to medium-high heat.
2. In a large mixing bowl, toss the trimmed green beans with olive oil until evenly coated.
3. Place the green beans in a grill basket or on a piece of aluminum foil.
4. Grill the green beans over indirect heat for 10-12 minutes, stirring occasionally, or until they are tender and slightly charred.
5. While the green beans are grilling, heat a small skillet over medium heat. Add the minced garlic and cook for 1-2 minutes, or until fragrant.
6. Stir in the barbecue sauce and cook for an additional 1-2 minutes, stirring occasionally, until the sauce is heated through.
7. Once the green beans are done grilling, transfer them to a serving dish.
8. Drizzle the barbecue sauce mixture over the grilled green beans and toss until they are evenly coated.
9. Season the BBQ green beans with salt and pepper to taste. If desired, sprinkle with crushed red pepper flakes for heat or top with sliced almonds or chopped bacon for added texture.
10. Serve the BBQ green beans hot as a delicious and flavorful side dish at your BBQ.

Enjoy the smoky flavor and tender texture of these BBQ green beans alongside your favorite BBQ meats and other sides!

Grilled Okra

Ingredients:

- 1 pound fresh okra pods
- 2 tablespoons olive oil
- Salt and pepper to taste
- Optional: Cajun seasoning, garlic powder, lemon juice

Instructions:

1. Preheat your grill to medium-high heat.
2. Rinse the okra pods and pat them dry with paper towels. Trim off the stem ends, but leave the pods whole.
3. In a large mixing bowl, toss the okra pods with olive oil until evenly coated.
4. Season the okra pods with salt and pepper to taste. If desired, sprinkle with Cajun seasoning or garlic powder for added flavor.
5. Place the okra pods directly on the preheated grill grates. Grill for 4-5 minutes on each side, or until they are tender and slightly charred.
6. Once the okra pods are done grilling, remove them from the grill and transfer them to a serving dish.
7. Optionally, squeeze fresh lemon juice over the grilled okra for a bright and tangy flavor.
8. Serve the grilled okra hot as a delicious and unique side dish at your BBQ.

Enjoy the smoky flavor and tender texture of grilled okra alongside your favorite BBQ meats and other sides!

Caprese Pasta Salad

- Optional: Balsamic glaze for drizzling

Instructions:

1. Cook the pasta according to the package instructions until al dente. Drain and rinse the cooked pasta under cold water to cool it down.
2. In a large mixing bowl, combine the cooked pasta, halved cherry tomatoes, diced fresh mozzarella cheese, and thinly sliced fresh basil leaves.
3. In a small bowl, whisk together the extra virgin olive oil, balsamic vinegar, salt, and pepper until well combined.
4. Pour the dressing over the pasta salad and toss until everything is evenly coated.
5. Taste the salad and adjust the seasoning if needed.
6. Cover the bowl and refrigerate the Caprese pasta salad for at least 30 minutes to allow the flavors to meld together.
7. Before serving, give the salad a final toss to redistribute the dressing and ingredients.
8. Optionally, drizzle balsamic glaze over the top of the Caprese pasta salad for extra flavor and presentation.
9. Serve the Caprese pasta salad cold as a delicious and refreshing side dish at your BBQ.

Enjoy the vibrant flavors and textures of this Caprese pasta salad alongside your favorite BBQ meats and other sides!

BBQ Bruschetta

Ingredients:

- 1 French baguette, sliced into 1/2-inch thick rounds
- 2 tablespoons olive oil
- 2 cups cherry tomatoes, diced
- 2 cloves garlic, minced
- 1/4 cup fresh basil leaves, thinly sliced
- 1 tablespoon balsamic vinegar
- Salt and pepper to taste

Instructions:

1. Preheat your grill to medium-high heat.
2. Brush both sides of the baguette slices with olive oil.
3. Grill the baguette slices on the preheated grill for 1-2 minutes on each side, or until they are lightly toasted and have grill marks. Remove them from the grill and set aside.
4. In a medium mixing bowl, combine the diced cherry tomatoes, minced garlic, thinly sliced fresh basil leaves, balsamic vinegar, salt, and pepper. Toss until everything is well combined.
5. Spoon the tomato mixture over the grilled baguette slices, dividing it evenly among them.
6. Optionally, drizzle a little extra olive oil over the top of each bruschetta for added flavor.
7. Serve the BBQ bruschetta immediately as a delicious appetizer or side dish at your BBQ.

Enjoy the fresh flavors and crunchy texture of this BBQ bruschetta as a tasty starter for your BBQ feast!

Asian Slaw

Ingredients:

For the slaw:

- 4 cups shredded cabbage (green cabbage, red cabbage, or a combination)
- 1 cup shredded carrots
- 1/2 cup thinly sliced bell peppers (red, yellow, or orange)
- 1/4 cup thinly sliced green onions
- 1/4 cup chopped fresh cilantro
- 1/4 cup chopped peanuts or almonds (optional, for added crunch)

For the dressing:

- 3 tablespoons rice vinegar
- 2 tablespoons soy sauce or tamari
- 1 tablespoon sesame oil
- 1 tablespoon honey or maple syrup (for vegan version)
- 1 clove garlic, minced
- 1 teaspoon grated fresh ginger
- Salt and pepper to taste
- Optional: Sriracha or chili paste for heat

Instructions:

1. In a large mixing bowl, combine the shredded cabbage, shredded carrots, thinly sliced bell peppers, sliced green onions, chopped fresh cilantro, and chopped peanuts or almonds (if using).
2. In a small bowl, whisk together the rice vinegar, soy sauce or tamari, sesame oil, honey or maple syrup, minced garlic, grated ginger, salt, and pepper until well combined. If desired, add Sriracha or chili paste to taste for some heat.
3. Pour the dressing over the slaw mixture and toss until everything is evenly coated.
4. Taste the slaw and adjust the seasoning if needed.

5. Cover the bowl and refrigerate the Asian slaw for at least 30 minutes to allow the flavors to meld together.
6. Before serving, give the slaw a final toss to redistribute the dressing and ingredients.
7. Serve the Asian slaw cold as a delicious and crunchy side dish at your BBQ.

Enjoy the fresh and vibrant flavors of this Asian slaw alongside your favorite BBQ meats and other sides!

Grilled Fennel

Ingredients:

- 2 fennel bulbs
- 2 tablespoons olive oil
- Salt and pepper to taste
- Optional: Lemon zest, chopped fresh herbs (such as parsley or dill)

Instructions:

1. Preheat your grill to medium-high heat.
2. Trim the stalks and fronds from the fennel bulbs. Cut each bulb in half lengthwise, then cut each half into wedges, keeping the core intact to hold the wedges together.
3. In a large mixing bowl, toss the fennel wedges with olive oil until evenly coated.
4. Season the fennel wedges with salt and pepper to taste. If desired, sprinkle with lemon zest and chopped fresh herbs for added flavor.
5. Place the fennel wedges directly on the preheated grill grates, cut side down.
6. Grill the fennel wedges for 4-5 minutes on each side, or until they are tender and lightly charred.
7. Once the fennel wedges are done grilling, remove them from the grill and transfer them to a serving platter.
8. Serve the grilled fennel hot as a delicious and aromatic side dish at your BBQ.

Enjoy the sweet and caramelized flavor of grilled fennel alongside your favorite BBQ meats and other sides!

Greek Salad Skewers

Ingredients:

- Cherry tomatoes
- Cucumber, cut into cubes
- Kalamata olives, pitted
- Feta cheese, cut into cubes
- Red onion, cut into small wedges
- Olive oil
- Lemon juice
- Dried oregano
- Salt and pepper
- Wooden skewers

Instructions:

1. Soak wooden skewers in water for about 30 minutes to prevent them from burning on the grill.
2. Thread cherry tomatoes, cucumber cubes, Kalamata olives, feta cheese cubes, and red onion wedges onto the skewers, alternating the ingredients as desired.
3. In a small bowl, whisk together olive oil, lemon juice, dried oregano, salt, and pepper to make a simple dressing.
4. Drizzle the dressing over the assembled skewers, coating them evenly.
5. Preheat a grill or grill pan over medium-high heat.
6. Grill the skewers for 2-3 minutes on each side, or until the vegetables are slightly charred and the cheese begins to soften.
7. Remove the skewers from the grill and transfer them to a serving platter.
8. Optionally, sprinkle the skewers with additional dried oregano and serve with extra lemon wedges on the side.
9. Serve the Greek salad skewers as a flavorful appetizer or side dish at your BBQ.

Enjoy the fresh and tangy flavors of these Greek salad skewers!

BBQ Rice Pilaf

Ingredients:

- 1 cup long-grain white rice
- 1 3/4 cups vegetable or chicken broth
- 1 tablespoon olive oil
- 1 small onion, finely chopped
- 2 cloves garlic, minced
- 1/2 cup diced bell pepper (any color)
- 1/2 cup diced carrots
- 1/2 cup frozen peas
- 1 teaspoon smoked paprika
- 1/2 teaspoon dried thyme
- Salt and pepper to taste
- Chopped fresh parsley for garnish (optional)

Instructions:

1. Rinse the rice under cold water until the water runs clear. Drain well and set aside.
2. In a large skillet or saucepan, heat the olive oil over medium heat. Add the chopped onion and sauté for 2-3 minutes until softened.
3. Add the minced garlic to the skillet and cook for an additional 1 minute until fragrant.
4. Stir in the diced bell pepper and carrots, and cook for 3-4 minutes until they begin to soften.
5. Add the rice to the skillet and cook, stirring frequently, for 2-3 minutes until the rice is lightly toasted.
6. Pour the vegetable or chicken broth into the skillet and bring to a boil.
7. Reduce the heat to low, cover the skillet, and simmer for 15-20 minutes, or until the rice is tender and the liquid is absorbed.
8. Stir in the frozen peas, smoked paprika, dried thyme, salt, and pepper, and cook for an additional 2-3 minutes until the peas are heated through.
9. Remove the skillet from the heat and let the rice pilaf sit, covered, for 5 minutes.
10. Fluff the rice pilaf with a fork and transfer it to a serving dish.

11. Garnish the BBQ rice pilaf with chopped fresh parsley, if desired, and serve hot as a delicious and flavorful side dish at your BBQ.

Enjoy the smoky flavors and hearty texture of this BBQ rice pilaf alongside your favorite grilled dishes!

www.ingramcontent.com/pod-product-compliance
Lightning Source LLC
LaVergne TN
LVHW081318060526
838201LV00055B/2335